Immortal Sofa

## Also By Maura Stanton

*Poetry*
Glacier Wine (2001)
Life Among the Trolls (1998)
Tales of the Supernatural (1988)
Cries of Swimmers (1984)
Snow On Snow (1975)

*Fiction*
Cities in the Sea (2003)
Do Not Forsake Me, Oh My Darling (2002)
The Country I Come From (1988)
Molly Companion (1977)

# Immortal Sofa

*Poems by*
*Maura Stanton*

University of Illinois Press

Urbana and Chicago

Library of Congress Cataloging-in-Publication Data
Stanton, Maura.
Immortal sofa : poems / by Maura Stanton.
p.   cm. — (Illinois poetry series)
ISBN 978-0-252-03308-7 (cloth : acid-free paper)
ISBN 978-0-252-07580-3 (pbk. : acid-free paper)
I. Title
PS3569.T3337I46     2008
811'.54—dc22     2008002075

For Richard
And for the Immortals O. and O.

# Acknowledgments

Grateful acknowledgment is made to the following magazines and anthologies in which these poems first appeared.

*Atlanta Review:* "Letter to the Old Magician"
*The Bellingham Review:* "Stare-e-o Vision Postcards"
*Caffeine Destiny:* "Through the Dark"
*Calapooya:* "Poem on a Forbidden Subject"
*The Cincinnati Review:* "Lost and Found"
*The Formalist:* "Dream Kitchen"
*ForPoetry.com:* "Dead Moth in a Bottle of Mineral Water"
*Harpur Palate:* "Greed"
*The Journal:* "Cimetière Virtual"
*Many Mountains Moving:* "At the Vet's," "Practicing T'ai Chi Ch'uan"
*Margie:* "Meditation while Cooking Soup"
*Mid-American Review:* "Translating"
*Nightsun:* "The Gilles"
*Orchid:* "Food Shows," "A Description of Our Morning"
*Ploughshares:* "Milk of Human Kindness"
*PN Review:* "Ode to Pokeweed"
*Poetry:* "A Night in Assisi"
*Prairie Schooner:* "Cocktail Glasses"
*Pool:* "Twenty Questions"
*River Styx:* "God's Ode to Creation," "Vacations in America"
*Salamagundi:* "Abstract Art"
*Shade:* "Immortal Sofa"
*Southwest Review:* "Tatyana"
*Third Coast:* "Psalm for a Lost Summer"
*Tin House:* "Pride and Prejudice: The Game"

"God's Ode to Creation" appeared on *Poetry Daily* (poetrydaily.com) and on *Verse Daily* (versedaily.com); "Translating" appeared on *Poetry Daily* (poetrydaily.com) and was reprinted in *The Best American Poetry 2003,* ed. David Lehman and Yusef Komunyakaa; "Twenty Questions" was reprinted in *The Best American Poetry 2005,* ed. David Lehman and Paul Muldoon; "Practicing Tai Chi Ch'uan" was reprinted in *Poets of the New Century,* David R. Godine, and in *Hammer and Blaze,* University of Georgia Press; "At the Vet's," "Dead Moth in a Bottle of Mineral Water," "Tatyana," and "A Night in Assisi" were also reprinted in *Hammer and Blaze.*

# Contents

# Immortal Sofa

*Part 1*

# God's Ode to Creation

# Nineteenth-Century Animals

*glimpsed in the memoirs of Marianne North
world traveler, painter, botanist*

In Jamaica two sheep
    Stand on their hind legs to beg for sugar.
A snail the size of a French roll crosses
    The road in Brazil, and lives in a foot-pan
For a month, eating green leaves. In swampy Illinois
    A cat drags a snake home to feed her kittens,
While on the train to Canada, a large tomcat
    Sits on a girl's knee, panting with its tongue out,
"every now and then giving most dismal mews."
    Fourteen elephants, forced to attend the opening
Of the new waterworks they'd helped build
    In Ceylon, moan during the long speeches
Afraid they'll slip down the hill in the mud.
    Outside Petropolis, as Miss North paints the view,
Tiny flies touch her freshly painted skies,
    Carrying off bits of blue on their wings.
Later there's "a spider as big as a small sparrow
    With velvety paws"
And monkeys who steal her paintbrush in India.
    At Niagara Falls, a dead workhorse on the road—
His friend, a black dog, nestles and whines,
    Tears in his soft brown eyes, tail tucked tight.
In New South Wales an opossum
    Laps milk out of a teaspoon while in Rajputana,
Hunting cheetahs chained to trestle-beds
    Watch prancing peacocks. On shipboard
A big monkey sits in the captain's armchair
    "reading Shakespeare." When she's bored
Miss North sews 2000 beetle wings to a piece of silk

the colors "more marvelous than the sea at Aden,
and every wing taking three stitches."
     Cobras dance to magic piping in Bombay,
And in Honolulu she buys two lei
     To pull apart as fodder for her three pet mice.
Her host in Queensland remembers Mr. Darwin
     Stopping by in the *Beagle,* so agreeable,
But "the ugliest young man he ever met."
     I read on and on, unable to stop myself
From combing these words, like thick grasses,
     For the uncanny fireflies with two green lanterns
On their foreheads, a red one on their tails.
     I wonder if the guinea per year subscribers
To *Mudie's Select Library (Limited)*
     *30 to 34 New Oxford Street,* stamped on Vol. I,
got excited over the black frog with garnet eyes
     and the whales swimming among the icebergs?
Inside these pages of incessant chatter
     Hundreds of cockatoos still screech and gossip,
And a mongoose eats both buttered toast and snakes.

# Translating

What are the characters eating in this novel
published in Barcelona in 1901
that I found this summer in my rented house?
It's raining hard. I've nothing else to read,
so I'm struggling with my high school Spanish.
What's *gragea*? *Cassell's Spanish Dictionary*
tells me it's a small, colored *bonbon*,
but, couched in odd British English,
other words make no sense. Two characters
walk through a plantation of *guindo* trees,
but when I look up the word, I see it means
*mazzard* in English. I read another page
almost understanding the stiff dialogue
until one character starts talking about
*humazga,* translated as *hearth-money,* or *fumage.*
What's that? An offering to the gods,
or the cost of fuel? *Cassell's* falls open
on my lap, and my eye skims down the columns
discovering that we lack words in English for
all kinds of stuff that happens everyday,
the act of doffing the hat, hunting with ferrets,
and the prick of stubble in a horse's eye,
that there are many things we've never named
properly, like tubes for sampling sherry,
large bushy wigs, cakes kneaded with oil,
deadly carrots, and large, uneven teeth.
I close the book, then notice a little *salton,*
or *grasshopper,* clinging to the window ledge,
his hind legs folded, waiting for the sun
just like me. I look up *boredom.*

Why, the word doesn't exist.
And, really, why would anyone wish for it
when there's *borecale* and *boree,* English words
I've never even heard of before, but defined
in Spanish, one a *cabbage,* the other a *dance.*

# Dead Moth in a Bottle of Mineral Water

Before you pour me down the kitchen sink
or else return my bottle to the store,
let me explain. It's true I ruined your drink
but not on purpose. You see I meant to soar
on new lavender wings when I hatched out
from sticky larvae. I dreamed of wild nights
fluttering over the trees, floating about
the wide world so I could see great sights.
At last my body changed. Now for the fun.
I rustled my antennae, enraptured by
a bright glow I thought was the glorious sun
and flew straight up, not knowing I would die
fried by a light bulb moments after birth
inside a bottling plant, my sparkling earth.

# Food Shows

Ever put ginger in an apple pie? No, I say.
My roommate's chattering behind a curtain.
She's watching food shows on her television,
A morphine drip in her arm just like mine.
Sometimes a nurse switches the curtains back
And I see a hand basting a fat chicken
Or a chef stirring a pot. Then my view's gone
But not her commentary. Oh, he's putting
Caviar in the scrambled eggs! Ever taste caviar?
No, I never have. Have you? Petroleum jelly!
Oh, my, what a great basket of persimmons,
Perfect for puddings, but I never ate
Persimmon cake before, did you? Nope, never.
And I never knew there were so many food shows
On all day, one following another, either,
I say, and she says, why, the only good thing
About being here is getting to watch them all,
Cuisine from New Orleans, Country Cookin',
The Italian, Chinatown and Napa Kitchens,
Even Baking Bread with Father Dominic.
That's albatross they're stuffing now, she cries,
But I'm already drifting into sleep
Where after-images of anesthesia
Etch my eyelids, swirling blobs and zigzags
Left over from the pain I didn't feel
Even as my brain stored the pulsations
Of nerves twanging under the surgeon's knife.
Ever mix angel hearts with wild mushrooms?

Ever stir baby's breath into soufflés?
Did I say yes or no? Now she's telling me
It's best to soak the tough thighs of naiads
In champagne before stewing. That fingernails
Of great pianists make a sparkling crust.

# Stare-e-o Vision Postcards

The pattern looks abstract, like rosy tweed
Or shag carpet. Stare hard into the dots.
Diverge your eyes. Look at the reflection
Cast on a window pane, then out beyond it.
Now focus on the postcard. Soon you'll see
A figure floating above the background
In three dimensions. No, you're not dreaming.
It's just your brain transforming the dots
Into depth cues, so that a dinosaur
Jaws open, claws extended, seems to jump
Out of the earth where it's been hidden
From ordinary sight. Here's the next card.
It looks like the spin-painting you once made
At the county fair, all splotches and streaks,
But hold it up before your eyes and wait
For buried shapes to form, detach themselves,
And loom out of the swirl of randomness.
See how a snow-capped mountain rises up
Against the speckled texture of the sky.
You almost think you could step inside
The frame, and enter the illusory space,
A knapsack on your back, your heart drenched
With longing as you climb a path that twists
Out of sight. But as soon as you blink,
The mountain vanishes into the chaos
Of splattered color. And here's another card,
One that surprises you, for there's a scene
Already illustrated, a paradise
Of swaying palms and beach, hibiscus flowers.
All's clear and open to the casual glance.

Or is it? Scrutinize the ocean
Where the artist has controlled the variations
Of the brilliant, scattered daubs and dashes
That imitate green, foam-flecked water,
And when your eyes finally focus close
As far away, you'll go beneath the waves
To find the branching coral, red and brown,
A school of drifting, fringed jelly fish,
And on a rock, once empty, by the shore,
A mermaid sunning her rainbowed tail.
You put the cards down, excited, restless,
Wishing you could use this new technique
On everything, and learn to see below
The visible world whenever you wanted—
Skies full of dolphins, angels in the sea.
You look out your window. The trees toss,
Clouds pass overhead and sparrows flutter
Inside the tangled twigs of the old hedge,
Inscrutable as ever. You stare and stare,
And then you remember, *this* was the way
You learned to read when you were a child,
Turning the gilt pages of the Fairy Book
Slower and slower, trying to penetrate
The hidden kingdoms your mother described
At bedtime, when she lulled you to sleep.
You gazed into the large-type alphabet
Until first one word, then another, burst
Out of the thickets of print into images,
Like genies freed from their enchanted lamps.

# At the Vet's

The German shepherd can't lift his hindquarters
off the tiled floor. His middle-aged owner
heaves his dog over his shoulder, and soon
two sad voices drift from the exam room
discussing heart failure, kidneys, and old age
while a rushing woman pants into the office
grasping a terrier with trembling legs
she found abandoned in a drainage ditch.
It's been abused, she says, and sits down,
the terrier curled in her lap, quaking
as the memory of something bad returns and returns.
She strokes its ears, whispering endearments
while my two cats, here for routine checkups,
peer through the mesh of their old green carrier,
the smell of fear so strong on their damp fur
I taste it as I breathe. Soon the woman,
like the receptionist with her pen in mid-air,
is listening, too, hushed by the duet
swelling in volume now, the vet's soprano
counterpointed by the owner's baritone
as he pleads with her to give him hope, the vet
trying to be kind, rephrasing the truth
over and over until it becomes a lie
they both pretend to accept. The act's over.
His dog's to stay behind for ultrasound
and kidney tests, and the man, his face
whipped by grief as if he were caught in a wind,
hurries past us and out the front door,
leaving the audience—cats, terrier, people—
sunk in their places, too stunned to applaud.

# Practicing T'ai Chi Ch'uan

From where I waver in the tall mirror
shaping my arms and legs into the postures
of the photographs, I see I've got them wrong.
I'll never learn *Deflect, Parry and Punch,*
*Strike with Palm and Descend,* or *Kick with Right Heel.*
But then I come across *White Crane Spreads Wings*
and imagine gliding high above my town,
headed south out over the reservoir
casting a shadow. Suddenly I see
how other movements may be hidden inside
my body like paper ready to be unfolded.
*Grasp the Bird's Tail. Wave Hands Like Clouds.*
I sweep my arms first this way, and then that,
watching a sleek crow dive past my window
as I shift left and right. Here's *Work at Shuttles.*
That's how I shop the grocery store each week,
Gliding dreamily behind my wire cart,
my fingers mechanically gathering stuff
though what they long to do is *Strum the Lute*
and fill the bright aisles with heavenly music.
The *White Snake Flicks Out Tongue.* I know
that quick hello from living in this town
for years, but where inside me is the skill
to *Part the Wild Horse's Mane?* I lift
my arms above my head, trying to remember
backwards through centuries to a seacoast
where a shadowy person with my DNA
saw the first hoof prints across the wet sand.

But it must have been aeons ago when something
slimy and quick, that evolved to be me,
learned to *Insert Needle to Sea Bottom.*
I close my eyes, trying to conjure the warm
watery planet, sizzling with lightning bolts,
where I darted and turned my somersaults
and then, diving through transparent depths,
inserted myself through the waving seaweed
and came back up, my eye filled with joy.

# A Description of Our Morning

Our morning always starts with sleepy sex
followed by cats and coffee, and lots of talk
remembering far off places. Once again
we resolve to stay as happy as this all day.

But we never do. Once out of our warm bed,
we're stuck with here, not there, our narrow closet
crammed with costumes, deep frowns, averted eyes,
downturned mouths, hunched shoulders, heavy shrugs

that let us blend in with all the locals.
My iron shoes, stacked in boxes, seem to grow
heavier with every step, your shaving cream
acidifies your skin with a burning flush

that might be anger, or the red of chagrin.
So just before we rise to daily life,
we lean back, petting the cats, eating muffins
dreaming of the country we call there.

There the native costume is a flashing smile,
bare feet, and flowing hair, and glowing eyes.
There the heart is not a bitten apple core
but a tender melon, sweet and sentimental.

But here's your grim lip-tightener, my dear,
and here, my darling, don't forget to slip
this fist into your pocket. Thanks. And here's
a box of sighs to stuff into your purse

for use at work. Sweetheart, don't forget
that cloak of gloom, the weather's sure to turn.
And please hand me my coat of many shadows
so I can dress for misery in grand style.

# Pride and Prejudice: The Game

When my youngest sister broke her right foot,
   she hobbled about her townhouse on crutches
unable to drive or go to work, eating frozen dinners
   but getting to read all the novels by Jane Austen
for the third or fourth time. She loves *Pride and Prejudice*
   so for Christmas I bought her *Pride and Prejudice: The Game*
and now we're sitting around her dining room table

   with my other sisters, looking at the colored board
printed with squares leading from one country house to another,
   along which we must move our cardboard figures,
trying to get each pair to the Parish Church to win.
   Ellen, with her broken foot, claims Elizabeth and Darcy,
Graciously, we let Jane take Jane and Mr. Bingley,
   while Honey, coughing hard because she has bronchitis,

says, *I'll be Lydia, at least Mr. Wickham's dashing*
   *even if he's unreliable* and I, since I'm the married sister,
already a winner, if this is how you win in this life,
   I settle for boring Charlotte and dreadful Mr. Collins
thinking too bad that Kitty and Mary have been left out
   of the official game just because they never married
at least inside the novel. *"Don't keep coughing so, Kitty,*

   *for heavens sakes!"* I could say to Honey
quoting Mrs. Bennet, if she'd been moving a Kitty figure
   along the board to Netherfield Park, but instead
the rest of us fall silent while she hacks and gasps
   exchanging worried looks, for she has asthma,
no sick days, and has to go on press checks at 3 A.M.
   for no overtime. "I do not cough for my own amusement,"

Kitty rebukes her mother, but she's only a minor sister,
     her prettiness leading nowhere, unlike stout Lydia
who married a cad. Then Jane throws the dice
     and the game begins! Mr. Bingley jumps five spaces
in the direction of Longbourn, Lizzie Bennet heads off
     another way to Pemberley, Honey moves Lydia
toward the soldiers' barracks, and I push Charlotte Lucas

     three spaces closer to the pompous idiot she preferred
to spinsterhood. And just then, my sister Sharon
     comes out from the kitchen where she's been gabbing
on her cell phone, and leans over the board
     admiring the drawings of the big English mansions
and we ask her to read the trivia cards that allow
     sudden swoops forward, or forfeits of a turn

and now we are five sisters bent over a miniature world
     all older than Jane Austen when she died at 41,
pretending to wear gloves and adore dances,
     trim hats, write chatty letters and play the pianoforte,
hoping to fill our dance cards, get invited for tea,
     though my sisters usually travel by freeway
in their own cars, singing along to the Beatles or Bob Dylan

     or rehearsing how they'll ask for the next raise
from an asshole boss, or counting frequent flyer miles
     to see if they can get to Hawaii next March,
wondering if there's anything in the freezer for supper,
     or if they should stop at the gym to lift weights
on the way home to large, bright rooms filled with plants,
     litter boxes, neat closets, and large screen TVs.

# Through the Dark

Word goes out over CB radios,
Over car phones, over emergency call boxes.
Truckers pull over, police cruisers wailing around them
Followed by fire trucks, ambulances, the SWAT team.
Traffic slows, halts. Motorists jump out
Chasing camera crews, and now it's LIVE
On television, and in the Sportsman's Bar
Men crane away from amber beers on the counter
To watch the small set fixed high on the wall,
Observing the flare-lit faces of onlookers
Roped off at the scene, and straining to hear
What's happening, what does all this mean?
My husband arrives at the Interstate entrance
To find traffic stopped, but a trucker gets out
Coming back to warn him before he's trapped—
"A lady's shot her husband. Turn around."
And so he's home, only ten minutes late,
Having taken a back route through cornfields.
I go to sleep thinking about that Interstate
My husband drives in the dark once a week,
His small car weaving in and out among
Shadowy semis heading south for Atlanta
Loaded with machine parts, or lengths of pipe,
And all those other cars driven by men and women
Heading somewhere, too, alert or sleepy,
Everyone watching the tail lights up ahead—
Yet every now and then someone's out there
Gripping the wheel, face a burning wound,
Chest full of rocks. Did that lady keep
A pistol in her purse, or turn in desperation

To grab a hunting rifle from the gun rack
Of her husband's pick-up, unable to take
Any more of something? But our story was garbled.
Next day the newspaper explains the truth,
How a young woman wanted to kill herself,
Depressed because her fiance had cheated.
And so she stopped her car in the center lane,
Holding a pistol to her head. No one
Could talk her out of it—she knew her life
Was over—why not die?—until the SWAT team
Filled her car with flash grenades and tear gas
And hauled her away, alive, on a stretcher.
Truckers, who'd sat in their rigs for hours
Catching up on paperwork, began to inch forward,
The choir got back on the church bus,
Drivers pulled off at gas stations to call home
And tell someone who answered on the first ring
Hey, I'm OK. And the divorced mother,
Delayed three hours, her grocery bags wet
From melted ice cream and thawed vegetables,
Hallelujahed the exit for her subdivision.

# God's Ode to Creation

"'Now there shall be tum-tiddly-um, and tum-tiddly-um,
  hey-presto! scarlet geranium!'"
  —D. H. Lawrence

Today's the kind of day when I feel good
about that dazzling stuff I've made down there,
everything so mixed up that even lies
turn out to be the truth. The legendary
amaranth, for example, somebody insists
they saw it growing down in Hell, and presto!
not only does it have a genus, and seeds,
but a real chemical formula so everyone
can dye their underwear dark purplish red.
You give me credit for the natural,
flame trees, tansy, sleek dangerous leopards,
and even tiny mites like the golden neotode
worming down into the rich potato plant,
the jerboa, the zoon, and the stargazer perch,
but I'm the author of the artificial, too,
those bolts of homespun Khaddar cloth, and guns,
concertos by Mozart, and tiny micro chips.
I've always loved the way the invisible
gets to be visible, my big winds measured
by the Beaufort Scale, so that a sailor
blown off course by Force 11 knows
the velocity of the storm that downed his ship
and understands, as he slowly starves to death
on a rocky desert island without coconut palms,
that the time between new moons, lunation,
is divided into 29 days, 12 hours,
44 minutes and 2.8 seconds.
                    What glorious precision!

It's too bad, I know you're thinking, that my rules
don't allow me to help that sunburned sailor
and I do regret that a Java sparrow didn't drop
some seeds from the mainland two centuries ago
so that a bunch of fruit trees could take root.
No need to impute malevolence to me,
or even indifference, for I feel bad
about what happens most days, looking down
at another execution in Huntsville,
sighing over another quake in Turkey.
But today the blue planet, wreathed in clouds,
looks extra lovely as it spins through space,
and I want a little praise for my handiwork,
my fleecy altocumulus, my silvery mists,
even that fancy stuff you built for me,
pagodas, skyscrapers, the Eiffel Tower.
Prayers are rare these days, instead I get
millions of poems constructed out of words
that sizzle in three thousand languages,
a few of them paeans, but most ironic jabs.
But do I zap the ones who mock? I don't.
At night I see them sweat and yearn, dreaming
of that one thing I never made, and won't.

*Part II*

# Lost and Found

# Lost and Found

A mile from home, I find the plastic bag
torn off my mums by last night's cold front wind.
It clings to chain link, one corner still knotted,
a deflated ghost. I pluck it off the fence,
thinking of lots of things I've lost forever.
What if they all came back this easily?
And I imagine a reverse tornado
roaring overhead straight to my house
and dumping everything on me at once.
First all the pairs of shoes I've ever worn—
my green spike heels, red sneakers, Buster Browns,
pumps, flats, wedges, thongs, and sandals
all piled on the lawn next to Christmas sweaters
and snowflake mittens. And all brand-new!
Over here's my bike, a blow-up kiddie pool,
boxes of mystery novels, a bassinet,
my stolen jewelry box, and the blue bikini
I wore in Nice when I was twenty-two.
The tree branches are full of board games,
Monopoly and Clue and Chutes and Ladders.
My paint-by-numbers rests on the hard black sofa
where I sat drinking Gallo Rhinegarten
on Church Street, and here's the fondue pot
that caught fire—everything's mine again
and I dig through mounds and heaps and piles
of clothes I'd forgotten, suitcases, dolls,
waving at people who pass on the sidewalk
thinking this is the season's biggest yard sale—
"No, this is all mine!"—rooting again,
amazed at the great hill of belongings, wondering

where I'll put all this stuff now that it's back.
But I'm busy swinging my old tennis racket,
trying on mini-skirts, calling my dog—
make that plural—for all three of them are here
though they really succeeded each other,
Casey and Casey II and Skipper,
dashing around in the spoils, barking happily.
Then I notice my father stumbling over
a load of toasters and coffee makers,
and stopping thoughtfully, just as he did in life,
to clean his glasses after he notices
the shiny '72 Datsun on my roof;
so I step back to consider this big mess
that's blocking the front door of my house,
realizing that I'll never get back inside
where the present waits in quiet empty rooms
unless I abandon every single thing.

# Ode to Pokeweed

A strange plant rises below my retaining wall
    down in the neighbor's unkempt, weedy yard
growing taller and taller every day, scaring me
    because its rhubarb-colored stems shoot up
against my deck, leaves the size of sugar scoops,
    and by midsummer glistening white berries
grow in clusters, slowly turning deep purple.
    I'm sure they must be poisonous, and I worry
about the hummingbirds and yellow finches.
    Wearing thick gloves, I hack at the plant.
Two days later it's grown back even denser,
    branches and shoots touching my deck rail
as the plant looms over the rose-of-Sharon bushes.
    I've never seen a weed this big in the city
so I search Web sites until I locate a picture
    of reddish stems and black berry bunches—
Why, you're pokeweed! Common old pokeweed!
    My grandfather cut you out of tobacco rows
down in Kentucky, whacking you away from fences
    where cows might browse, accidentally brushing
swollen udders over your poisonous leaves.
    I'd work the pump lever while he washed
your purple stains off his hands, cursing you
    for making trouble. But Pokeweed, you're not
all bad, in fact, you're an American classic
    with many nicknames, some fond, some cruel,
and once upon a time you fed the roaring waves

of passenger pigeons that crowded the sky.
    They called you pigeon berry then, though others
who noticed bears feasting in late summer
        named you bear's grape. Thoreau declared he'd like
your tall graceful stalk for a cane, while pioneers
        cooked and ate your tender early leaves,
labeling you American spinach, and even today
        you're canned and sold as poke salet,
*salet* being an old-fashioned word for cooked greens,
        though of course your roots, cooked or uncooked, can kill,
earning you another name, American nightshade.

    Garget, skoke, crowberry, cancer root—
you kept coming up everywhere, so naturally
        hungry people tasted your various parts,
cooking your stems (not a good idea),
        stuffing pokeberries into their mouths, getting sick
on your raw berries, baking pokeberry pies,
        everyone complaining how your berries stained
all they touched, so you became ink-
        berry, and quill pens scratched your dark juice
across ledgers and precious scraps of paper,
        and surely a lonely trapper or miller's wife
composed a secret poem out of your tincture.

    Then finally, to make you even more American,
you were noticed by speculators, entrepreneurs,
        and off your cuttings went to France and Italy.
Your squirty purple ooze colored cheap wine,
        turning pale grapes an enticing burgundy,
but also giving people queasy stomachs;
        and traveling English folk, in love with the exotic,
planted you in their gardens back home
        making you an ornamental, officially beautiful.

So all August I sat out on my deck, drinking tea,
    admiring you, volunteer pokeweed, a botanical treasure
with a long history, proud that you'd chosen
    to grow up in front of me like a tropical dream.
Poisonous to humans, but attracting wildlife,
    your berries feeding the robins and brown thrashers,
as well as bluebirds, cardinals, sapsuckers and Phoebes,
    and even mammals, like opossums and white-footed mice,
you're worth celebrating. The Algonquians
    named you "pakon," meaning "dye plant,"
and now researchers are even harvesting you for drugs
    that help HIV patients, so I feel lucky
that you manifested yourself right before my eyes
    with your great lineage, your cousinship with hoopvine
and the great Ombu tree of the Argentinean pampas.
    One night I went to a party in the summer twilight
and among the weeds edging my friend's patio
    I saw little pokeweeds with greenish berries
shimmering near the bare ankles of the women
    drinking wine, or dancing as the music blared,
and got so excited I started babbling and toasting you.
    For the first time since high school biology
I could name a wild plant! People thought I was crazy.
    But just today, two inches of steady, heavy rain
fell from a slow-moving tropical depression,
    and when I looked out my window—you were gone!
I got out my umbrella, and looking down
    discovered you beaten flat on the ground below,
your thick hollow stalks bent in the middle like knees,
    your big leaves tossed over like someone
washing their long hair in the kitchen sink.
    I felt like I'd lost my best friend, and leaned over
my deck rail, sick to my stomach, as if I'd eaten you.

But you'll be back, pokeweed. Perennial, you'll rise up
next spring, stronger than before, and the birds
    eating those purple berries will stain sidewalks
with new seeds, and more of you will poke up
    in the cracks between curbs, in vacant lots,
inside hedges, along the weedy margins of fences,
    and if my friend doesn't mow you down
she may discover you nodding over her patio next June
    some sunny day when we're both sitting around
drinking iced tea, talking about poetry.
    She'll look over at you, repulsed, frowning,
wondering what in the world you are, and I'll say, Pokeweed!

# Milk of Human Kindness

Tastes like the melted centers of toasted marshmallows. Tastes like tears of nectar squeezed out of clover blossoms. Tastes like sips from rivers running through lands of milk and honey. Remember those wax bottles filled with colored liquids, how as a child you bit off the top and sucked out the sweet purple, or red, or orange? You opened waxed cartons in the lunchroom, stuck in your straw, bubbled and gurgled. You loved chocolate best. So did your friends. And there was always enough to drink, more than you could finish. But now your mouth is dry. The milk of human kindness tastes like a punch in the nose. It tastes like phlegm, like snot. Tastes metallic like coins you don't give to homeless teenagers panhandling downtown, tastes like your blood-pressure medicine, tastes like a dry martini, tastes like the ring of soured froth in the cat's unwashed bowl, still sitting in the sink. She's meowing at the refrigerator door. She knows where you keep it.

# The Gilles

Tonight an invisible beam
from an orbiting satellite
transmits the news in French
down to my TV screen
here in the cold Midwest
on Shrove Tuesday. In Belgium
a woman stuffs straw from a bale
into an old man's coat,
turning him into a "Gilles,"
a clown in a bright costume
printed with rampant lions.
Beginning at four A.M.,
bells clanging from his belt,
he'll dance with hundreds of others
for twenty-four hours
through the streets of Binche,
and if you lived there
you'd see groups of Gilles
in white hoods, lace cuffs,
coming toward your house
like figures from a dream,
throwing oranges from baskets.
Three hundred thousand oranges,
the reporter says, showing
a shopkeeper rolling wire
over his plate glass window,
and I turn up the sound,
thinking I must have heard
the number wrong, my French
not good enough, but no

the sound of breaking glass
accompanies brass bands,
kettledrums and bells,
as the Gilles dance away demons
and bury the winter,
moving in packs through the village
down every street, pouring
at last into the square
where each Gilles carries
eight swaying ostrich feathers
on top of his head
for the closing ritual dance
measured to tabor and fife,
a dance commemorating
Pizarro's victory
over the Incas of Peru.
At the end of the news broadcast
I turn off my set, hearing
a sharp electric ping,
and then nothing but the wind
rattling my house like a drum.
I remember the empty ruins
of Machu Picchu
where I wandered as a tourist
touching the massive stones
and climbing dizzying staircases
above the Urubamba Gorge,
strangely unmoved by the Incas
who seemed like dinosaurs
vanished into books and museums.
But tonight something collides
in the air, or in my head,
for the wailing of the wind
scares me, as if those Gilles
rustling their straw chests
might be coming down my street

to show me what's below
every civilized nation,
dancing with slow steps
as they pause to look up
at my lighted window, their eyes
blank, archaic, and violent.

# Dear Listener, Dear Reader

Imagine Scyld's ship washing up on *your* shore, dear listener
(squatting there in your hut as the bard recites Beowulf).
Ring-prowed, gold sail in tatters, loaded with treasure,
You spot the ship stranded on the kelp at the tide line.
First you dump out the gull-bitten corpse,
Bury it, like smelly crab guts in a deep sand hole.
And then you stack up the goods there on the beach,
Near the spot where you'd been bashing seals to death.
You finger the damp strips of cloth of gold,
Pleased you can now swaddle your latest baby
So it won't cough and die like the other seven.
You count the big drinking vessels studded with rubies
Disappointed not to find a cask of mead,
And you admire the two large swords with silver hilts,
Testing the sharp blades on seal blubber, slash, slash!
Then you pull the plumed helmet over your head
Grinning to feel the heavy bowl warm your ears.
The old bard drones on, dragging the story forward
But you've heard it all before, every arctic winter,
And you tune him out, reveling in bright metals
Some sea-trader might exchange for sheepskins or beer.

Now the ring-prowed ship arrives at your shore, dear reader
(idly turning the crackling thin pages of the Norton Anthology).
But the sea-soaked planks, the broken mast, even the bones
Of the warrior-king wound up in his golden shroud,
And the piles of greenish rings and rusty spearheads,
Quaint mead cups, breast ornaments, unpolished swords
Don't interest you, with your Visa and Master-Card.

You walk along the sea-wracked tide line in Birkenstocks,
Looking out at the pale sea, the furrows of the waves,
And you exult, watching the sea-currents under black cliffs,
Sleek seal heads bobbing on the great sea-plain,
And mighty whales moving along the foam-flecked roads.
You take a long, deep breath of unpolluted air
Blowing over the frost-cold sea, counting as treasure
All fishes crowding the woven-waves, extinct seabirds
Gliding over the swan routes, and in the wolf-dark forests
Swift running hart measuring the miles of snowfall.
You pick up Scyld's helmet, hold it over your head
But it's too small to fit your large, evolved cranium
And you toss it down. It's too warm in this room
Where you sit reading, stroking the cat on your lap,
Bored by accounts of battles, dreaming of bad weather,
The great, heaving waves, the cries of gulls and curlews.

# Tatyana

She leaves the room. Onegin writhes
On stage, ashamed of his emotion.
He scorned her as a young girl.
Now he's mad about her! But she's
Married, rich, so stern and cold . . .
I lean forward in my opera seat.
There goes me. And isn't that
Every man I loved in vain?
The cast bows to wild applause.
Our Tatyana smiles, steps forward
To catch a bouquet of red roses.
I button my coat, grab my purse,
And make my slow way down the aisle
Of well-dressed, gray-haired couples
Watching their steps with downcast eyes.
I bet I'm not alone in wishing
I could go back in time, and break
A few cold hearts that broke mine
With all my hard-won understanding
Of the game of love, its rules
And stratagems, and power plays.
Then through the open lobby doors
Where the crowd hesitates, tying
Scarves or pulling on wool gloves,
I see the promised snow's begun
And someone's whistling an aria
From the first act. A sweet joy
Rushes through me. No, of course
I'd fall in love the same way.
I'd make every great mistake

I could, and earn this lovely moment
Walking home through fresh snow
My head full of unsingable music,
Remembering this one and that one
Who made me feel by feeling nothing.

# Twenty Questions

Who wrote *Heart of Darkness?* And what's the name
Of Dale Evan's horse? Why did thieves steal
Charlie Chaplin's corpse? Can you explain
Hieroglyphs in shells? How do you feel?
How many grains of (popcorn, rice, sand) fill
This container? Why did they auction off
Maria Callas's underwear? Would you like a pill?
Do you feel tired, perhaps? Is that bed soft?
Can you remember your parents' wedding date?
Your own? Like a glass of milk? Some champagne?
How many rhymes in a sonnet? Something you ate?
Who invented Bacos? Think it will rain?
Lie back now. Shall I bring you some chips?
What's the answer? It's rising to your lips.

# Poem on a Forbidden Subject

As I lean over the podium surveying two hundred bright blank faces enrolled in my Intro to Poetry Writing class, I hold up a small stuffed animal. It's the teddy bear that sits on my desk at home, a gift my brother gave me as a joke on my fiftieth birthday. I look at the class. I tell them Never, Do Not Ever (this semester) write a poem about a teddy bear—Do Not, Please, in long or short lines, describe any bear's torn ear (especially if it rhymes with dear), and don't extemporize over the glass eye hanging by a thread, the lumpy stuffing, the soiled plush, and the little bear heart beating deep. Then the class files out, some muttering about the way I'm stifling creativity, and I pack away my nameless teddy bear, dropping him down on my umbrella. But as I cross the campus, briefcase slung over my shoulder, I know my bear's in there struggling for air and feeling sad about my hard-heartedness towards helpless stuffed animals, and other victims I won't allow to enter the realm of feeling—like the sidewalk cruelly stretched under my feet, the grass crushed and sighing when I shortcut across it, and especially the floorboards in my living room, that creak as I stomp over them, each board dreaming about the forest in spring, remembering the sweet breeze and the chartreuse brightness of new leaves. I go out on my patio. Nature peers at me from many sad eyes, but I refuse to look back, just as I refuse to acknowledge the plastic pirate without legs that I stick in a geranium pot year after year, even though I know that all summer long he's trying to climb out of the dirt, and get back to his ship. And, yes, I wish he could reach that ship, and sail away among the clouds . . . the clouds passing over . . . here and there . . . those drifting clouds.

# A Night in Assisi

I rubbed my eyes. How strange I felt. It was
As if a fissure in my brain had opened
Spilling out dreams. I sat in a small cafe
On the Piazza del Commune, where laughing kids
Practiced skits for a religious pageant
Dressed like angels, saints, Mary, even Christ
Grinning through a false beard as he showed off,
And the Wolf of Gubbio prancing upright—
The same crew I'd seen in the famous frescos
Of the Basilica. At ten o'clock bells
Rang out. Shouting, laughing, bursting into hymns,
The kids formed into lines and marched off.
Now murmuring voices lulled me as I sipped.
Tourists gabbled over drinks at other tables
Comparing Italian truffles to French,
Giotto to Cimabue, Assisi to Urbino . . .
I was so sleepy I seemed to understand
Words in languages I didn't speak
So I got up, yawning, and wandered uphill
Thinking the view might please me. And it did.
Mist floated like flimsy curtains on a stage
Down in the valley, while up above the moon
Illuminated the medieval churches,
Belltowers, refectories, and carved facades.
I leaned on a parapet, remembering
How I'd played a friar in a parish play
About St. Francis preaching to the birds.
My mother cut out a pattern, and stitched
Brown cloth on her old Singer in that life
Of faith and miracles I'd led as a child.

I'd write J.M.J. on the top of my tests,
And each night kneel to pray beside my bed.
How solid religion seemed, like the great town
Lined with stone buildings a thousand years old
That I'd walked through on the way up, never
Suspecting that below me plates of rock
Scraped forward on a molten sea, heading
For a collision that would crack churches,
Turn plaster saints to rubble and paint chips,
And topple towers where bright bells had pealed.

# Psalm for a Lost Summer

1. By the rivers of Estes Park, there we sat down, yes, we sighed, when we remembered Italy.
2. We pressed our pens against paper, and we sat under the pine trees, listening to the crows.
3. For there in Colorado we were captive at a high altitude, required to write without breath; and if we could not write, our consciences required us to read, and improve our minds.
4. How shall we write our poems in this strange land?
5. If I forget you, Venice, let my right hand forget to wind the fettuccini around the fork.
6. If I do not remember balmy Sorrento, let me never taste lemons again; if I prefer not Capri above my chief joy.
7. Remember, O Muse, the couple who strolled about Assisi; who said, How lovely this is, but next year let's vacation at home.
8. O citizens of Assisi, do not blame us for the earthquake that destroyed your basilica; how happy we were, looking at your frescos during a thunderstorm.
9. Happy we shall be again, when we dash from this rented cabin, and drive down from these great stone mountains forever, Amen.

# Vacations in America

We huddle on the bed with our two cats.
There is no sun in the Wisconsin Dells.
The dripping forest hums with biting gnats.
All night we listen to some couple yell.

There is no sun in the Wisconsin Dells.
A trucker plays guitar in the next room.
All night we listen to some couple yell.
A forty watt bulb scatters rays of gloom.

A trucker plays guitar in the next room.
We leave Utah before the free doughnuts.
A forty watt bulb scatters rays of gloom.
Who filled the toilet with cigarette butts?

We leave Utah before the free doughnuts.
In Florida a loud TV keeps us awake.
Who filled the toilet with cigarette butts?
This paid reservation was a mistake.

In Florida a loud TV keeps us awake.
Who ever thought South Bend could be so cold?
This paid reservation was a mistake.
The nicer places won't take cats, we're told.

Who ever thought South Bend could be so cold?
A prostitute knocks on the battered door.
The nicer places won't take cats, we're told.
A file of red ants crosses the bathroom floor.

A prostitute knocks on the battered door.
A TV tuned to static makes white noise.
A file of red ants crosses the bathroom floor.
Deep in Dixie, whoops from good old boys.

A TV tuned to static makes white noise.
Close the curtain gap with a safety pin.
Deep in Dixie, whoops from good old boys.
The walls are too thin at the Roadway Inn.

Close the curtain gap with a safety pin.
All night the lovers rock their noisy bed.
The walls are too thin at the Roadway Inn.
Forget the sex stains on the flowered spread.

All night the lovers rock their noisy bed.
Montana serves up stacks of rubber pancakes.
Forget the sex stains on the flowered spread.
Why do hikes always end at buggy lakes?

Montana serves up stacks of rubber pancakes.
Upend the mattress so the cat climbs out.
Why do hikes always end at buggy lakes?
Are you sure AAA chose the best route?

Upend the mattress so the cat climbs out.
There's never any parking at the Viewpoint.
Are you sure AAA chose the best route?
This hellhole only has one pizza joint.

There's never any parking at the Viewpoint.
One of the cats is throwing up again.
This hellhole only has one pizza joint.
Each new place is just like where we've been.

One of the cats is throwing up again.
The dripping forest hums with biting gnats
Each new place is just like where we've been.
We huddle on the bed with our two cats.

*Part III*

# The Tale of Hermann Goertz

# The Tale of Hermann Goertz

Dublin, Ireland. Police Station
May 23, 1947. 10:30 A.M.


The mason looks around the dreary room
But no one glances up or calls his name
So he can pay his fine, get the hell out.
He's only twenty-one, but hates his life
Of dull workdays and even duller Sundays.
Police clerks glower over typewriters
Ignoring everyone, but soon an old man
Dressed in a dirty suit and wrinkled tie
Staggers out of the Aliens Office
And throws himself down hard on the bench
Next to him. "Is that lime dust," he asks,
"All over your boots? I know it well. You see,
I've broken my share of stones in this life, too."
He leans so close the mason see the flecks
Of grit stuck to his eyelashes, and the red
Stippled across the whites of his pale eyes.
"I'm Herman Goertz," the man says quietly.
"I'm a German spy. I've lived here seven years—
Four years in the internment camp at Athlone.
Since September I've been free, reading books
Of history in the National Library.
Now they're deporting me back to Berlin,
Handing me over as a prize to the Russians
Who'll torture me for a few names. But look!"
The mason sees a bit of shining glass
Clenched between his thumb and index finger.
"I still control my future. How about you?"
The mason shrugs. "I'd like to leave Dublin
And go to America." The old man laughs.

"People are funny. I once dreamed of Ireland
The way some boys imagine Arabia.
Miss Bishop taught me English in Lubeck.
She came from Ireland, preferred it to London
Where she'd gone as governess at sixteen.
She lulled me to sleep with her fairy tales
Of warriors, changelings, and magic springs.
We'd walk along the tide flats, and pretend
That fog bank out to sea was really Ireland.
Then I grew up to fight in the Great War.
A British shell smashed my leg. And look—"
He rolls his trouser leg to show the mason
A zigzag of pink scar. "I'm alive now
Only because of this. Bandaged, limping,
They sent me to teach at the flying school
In Schwaring, and I took Irish airmen
Up in my plane. We practiced reconnaissance
Over the hedgerows and rippling rye fields
And sometimes swung out over the Grey Sea
(The sea called the North Sea on English maps)
Scanning the steep dark waves for battleships.
Torn mist rushed past the wings, and lonely lights
Appeared next to the inky lines of rivers.
I think that was the happiest time of my life.
Landing, we'd cross the airfield like brothers,
Singing and shouting, arms around each other.

After the war, life was a shadow of life—
Gaunt-faced women begged in the streets to feed
Men reduced to legless heaps in barrows.
I studied law, entered my father's law firm
And took on clients who were bankrupt,
Suing for reparations from the British.
Of course I lost each case. I had no money.
At night I worked slowly on a novel
About two families ruined by the war,

One English, the other German like mine.
I titled it *Bridge Over the Grey Sea*
Remembering the way light fell in sheets
Of rain on the vast lawns of my boyhood,
And how I used to ride down the hard sand
At low tide, chasing after a rainbow.
But the debts grew faster than my pages,
And in '35 I tried to combine
The legal work with research on my novel.
I sailed for England with Marianne Emig,
An eager little blonde who took dictation.
We'd met on holiday. She called me "uncle."
We settled into a cottage in Broadstairs
And one day cycled to Manston Aerodrome
Past yellowing hayfields. The water meadows
Prickled like gooseflesh, and I made sketches
As she combed her hair, then spread a towel
For tea and strawberries. But I swear I didn't
Calculate the trajectory for bombers
As they claimed at my trial, but only pictured
My fictional airman standing where I stood
Catching the hum of planes taxiing down
The blistered tarmac. Marianne grew bored,
Jarred by a language she didn't understand;
I took her back to Hamburg, leaving my trunk,
And when I returned I was arrested
For spying, and all because my landlady
Rummaged until she found what she expected
Of any German, photographs and letters.

Nothing I'd done was even illegal!
But the motive they ascribed made me guilty.
Sentenced to four years in a British prison,
I chipped stone, like you do, to repair
The prison's heavy walls, or scrubbed floors,
Or slaved in the laundry over steaming vats.

Don't talk to me of Hell. I've been there,
Sweat streaming down my neck, my lungs burning,
My cracked hands bleeding as I stirred the sheets
Or raised a mallet over smoking granite
Beside poor Irishmen. At night I heard
Talk floating from the cells as lonely men
Reminisced about the far-off villages
Where they grew up, before the loot of London
Lured them first to factories, then to crime.
It seemed to me that I was one of them,
Exiled in a foreign country, hated because
Of where I came from, and the way I spoke.
At last, after three years I was sent home
For good behavior. At once I volunteered
For any mission Hitler chose for me,
And to my joy, I was to go to Ireland.

Failed lawyer, failed novelist—so be it!
They'd punished me for being what I wasn't,
So I'd succeed at being a great spy.
After weeks of training, learning to hide
A parachute, how to throw a grenade,
And how to best persuade the IRA
To attack Britain up on the border,
I finally floated down—into a bog!
I slogged through ferns and mud for hours
But couldn't find the parachute that carried
My radio, and had to swim a river.
I lost my map. I lost my invisible ink.
I hid in ditches, rushes, behind rocks,
Starving, getting sick on green blackberries
And when I met the IRA at last
I found I was the hero in a farce,
Or maybe one of Shakespeare's capering clowns
Singing hey-nonny through five tragic acts.
No one trusted me. No one believed

A submarine might surface late at night
Off the Dingle coast, if I could only get
A transmitter and contact Germany.
They hid me here and there for nineteen months,
Asking me for money I didn't have,
Sharing whiskey and bread, but never
Listening to me, only gabbing and gabbing
About somebody else in the next town
Who was the man I needed. But always
That man, when we met face to face, said no,
He wasn't the one, but he knew someone else
The man I really needed, and once again
I'd crouch under horse blankets, shipped
Off to god knows where, and find myself
Cowering in an attic or someone's back room
While an anxious woman tended the fire.
Once I tried to leave in a rubber boat
But the wind howled, and I turned back.
Next night the motor wouldn't start at all.

Finally they caught me in a police raid
By accident, and the Irish military
Interrogated me long days and nights,
Not understanding I was on the side
Of Ireland. I had to invent stories,
Use stratagems and ruses, making use
Of the artifices of a novelist
Though I had nothing to write on but the air,
No pen but my own voice sunk to hoarseness.
At last they sent me to rainy Athlone,
To that brick prison run by Commandant Power,
A name only an allegorist would choose
To give a jailor. And there I met
My detested fellow spies, all amateurs—
Salesmen, louts, gangsters, philosophers, fools—
Schutz with his two big ginger cats who kept

Vermin from his cell, and licked his plates:
Jan van Loon, the balding Dutch fascist;
Thick-necked Willy Preetz who'd cheerfully sell
His own mother for a pack of Chesterfields;
Hulking Unland yammering about Russia;
And Weber-Drohl, the chiropractor, always
Grabbing you by the shoulders for a quick snap;
And skinny Obed, who hated the British,
Making his curry messes out of peelings,
Insisting India was superior to Europe,
That someday everyone would agree with him
For time was endless. One day a policeman
Fished a dead swan out of the Shannon River,
And brought it to us as a joke, but Obed
Stuffed it with potatoes, roasted it black,
And ate it with gusto while the rest of us
Gagged in disgust. He wiped his mouth, laughing.
At how it was the "swan" we couldn't swallow,
Not the fowl, with its wings and webbed feet.
Words were illusions, he said, shimmering
Over things like a mist, obscuring sight.
Later, Preetz threw scalding tea in his face
Claiming he'd told the guards about the tunnel
We took turns digging in Van Loon's cell.

But Obed was right. Words are an illusion.
I'd spend hours composing in my code,
Describing a snail, or a wet windowpane,
Or the eyes of Kathleen Ni Houlihan
In rapturous detail, as if I were a poet,
Priding myself on the beauty and clarity
Of my public message, while underneath
I begged for a hacksaw baked in a cake
And a bicycle to escape from Athlone.
I gave each precious message to a guard
Who claimed to hate England, and each time

The coded reply appeared below the drainpipe
From the mysterious agent in Dublin,
"Must consult Berlin," I comforted myself
By thinking that somebody higher up
Would soon decipher all my clever words.
I'd reach a reader at the top who'd grasp
Everything I wanted, who could use
Scraps of information, odd bits of news
Gleaned from bridge games with the Commandant.
At last Germany asked for an account
Of all I'd done here before my capture,
And I wrote it with pleasure, eighty pages
Of lyric elegance covering the truth,
The contacts, dates, places I'd visited,
Groups I'd talked with and my analysis
Of Ireland's politics, and allegiances.
But it was only Irish intelligence
Toying with me. When the war ended
Officers took me for a pint and told me
Most kindly how I'd been duped for years,
All my efforts watched like a comedy.
What was I? Nothing. Nothing I'd ever done
Mattered at all. I moved to Dublin then,
And began to work for just a little money
With the Save the German Children Fund,
And when I had time, I read all I could
In the National Library, trying to
Displace the horror in my brain with facts
So I could sleep at night, not writhe and groan."

At last he pauses. But the mason's face
Is pale as stone. He stares straight ahead
At the glittering vial, and Goertz leans closer
"Let me ask you, how does a mason die?
He breaths in too much brick dust or else
Falls off scaffolding around a chimney.

Well, isn't this a suitable death for me—
The only proper death if I'm a spy?"
Swiftly he puts the vial into his mouth
And bites down. The bitter almond smell
Shocks the mason, who shouts for help,
And clerks and officers come running out.
But Goertz's skin is blue, his labored breath
Caught in his constricted throat. He doesn't
Hear the cries, the accusations, or feel
The fingers digging glass out of his mouth,
Or see the mason, stepping slowly back,
Grasping what he'll try to put in words
For the rest of his life, though no one listens,
His young face broken open like a geode.

*Part IV*

# Cimetière Virtual

# Oleander Cloud

*1981–2002*

Bird-like notes, punctuated by silence,
Floated like bubbles into our bedroom
The morning after Oleander died.
The meshed wire of the one-way screen
Let us see out, though no one could see in.
A jackrabbit browsed the dusty shrubbery
And two roadrunners flickered up the slope.
We listened to the tones of the *shakuhachi,*
The bamboo flute our neighbor played each dawn,
A piece he called "Tenderness of Cranes"
That imitates the trills of parent birds
Fussing over their young. Three years ago
He'd given up his silver flute to learn
Ancient melodies, and now he conjures
Doleful tones out of his breath before work
At the Sedona Coop, where he unpacks
Broccoli, fills bins with peppers and squash.

He hadn't changed. We watched him bike to work.
Oh, why couldn't we step through the thick wall
Of time itself, go back a day or two and shop
The Coop's cheerful aisles looking for stuff
That everyone buys, garlic or cat food?
Or go back further, hurry away from her death
To an earlier morning when she leapt across
My lap, stealing a bite of cinnamon doughnut,
Or rolled over for pets, purring and stretching?
But we had stepped into an empty room
Beyond her death, the way you might arrive

Jet-lagged in a strange hotel, your belongings
Spread out on the bed, crumpled, displaced.

We needed to buy a small urn—for her ashes—
And have it ready, the vet had told us,
So we drove to the only funeral home in town.
The receptionist sat before a fish tank
Gaudy with spangled fins and darting tails,
And when we said we wanted something small
For a cat's ashes, she called out the mortician.
He came smiling in his rolled-up shirt-sleeves,
Sweating, hearty. Said he needed dimensions
And when we looked at him in confusion,
Kindly called his brother-in-law at the pound
To ask how much was usually left to bury.
Then he'd showed us what he had for people
Taking us to a back room, past empty coffins.
We looked at wooden chests with brass plaques,
At ugly urns of brass or cloisonné,
Then turned the pages of a catalogue
Looking at crosses, jewelry boxes, lamp bases.
What could hold a small cat for eternity?

I shut the cover, handed back the book
Remembering Oleander's puzzled face
Watching me through the screen of her carrier
As we left the vet, hoping she'd wake up
From anesthesia her old hungry self.
How could that be yesterday? I could almost
Pull myself back over the sill of time,
Join her there, but the hours were growing thick
Between us like stacked bricks, dense, opaque.
And I thought of my last view of my father
Twelve years ago (though how could it be!),
Who stood waving goodbye from the back door,
Watching me through the screen as I pulled

Down the drive. Next time I saw his face
His eyes were closed, his pillow was satin,
His bed a coffin like the ones on display.
Now grief was doubled. We said thanks, goodbye.

Driving along the street, we passed signs
Selling crystals, Tarot cards, and prayer-wheels,
Tours to Vortex sites, psychic readings,
And séances where the dead could flock back
With messages and riddles for the living
Just as in the days of the Delphic Oracle
Or the witch of Cumae. If I longed
To hear that Oleander missed her life,
Still loved us, all I needed to do
Was hand some money to the channeler
Who advertised she spoke to animals
In the other world, and join those crowds
Of desperate Greeks and gullible Romans
Longing for a shape inside the smoke.
I laughed bitterly. I knew she was gone
Forever, didn't I? But as we hiked up
A steep trail above the desert, a cloud
Shaped just like her formed over my head,
Or out of my head, for the lines dissolved
As I lifted my arms, wild to snatch her
Out of the nothingness of the dry air.

# Letter to the Old Magician

"The aging magician retired to his island"
—Donald Justice (1925–2004)

Back when the sea was full of monsters
Your wand could turn clouds into Alps.
I remember my days as a young magician
Enthralled by your hypnotic voice.

All day I practiced my hocus-pocus,
Trying to tame a baby sea horse
While you made the waves stand still
And gathered pearls alongside mermaids.

Too soon my apprenticeship was over.
I waved goodbye, caught the ferry,
And found a cave on the crowded mainland,
Painting my ceiling with constellations

Just like yours. But lightning didn't flash
When I recited new fangled charms,
And though I wore real wizard's robes
And sat up late, no demons came

Shrieking up to do my bidding,
And weather never seemed to change.
How did you make those perfect runes?
I poured over your subtle spells

Trying to grasp the mysterious way
A simple hex could open Heaven—
And now and then I got it right:
A maple changed into a palm tree.

A unicorn leapt across the highway.
But years went by. My cloak frayed.
My voice shook as I explained
Incantations to my own pupils,

And made them practice old enchantments
Telling them stories of my youth
When genies slept in every lamp
And wishing caps were all the rage.

Dear Teacher, I meant to hoist a sail
And land again on your green island.
I dreamed of pacing the strand with you,
Talking of Merlin and of Comus

While the whales breached off shore.
But now comes news that there's no Justice
On earth. You who could conjure
Whole orchestras have fallen silent.

Now hurricanes will blow at random,
Spirits roam without direction,
Clouds are clouds, not mountain ranges,
And old students pace and mumble

Ancient abracadabra,
Trying to hex you back to life
From some unsatisfactory headland
Where the wind's too cold, no dolphins leap.

# Elegy for Olive

*1981–2003*

To write an elegy means you are dead.
You aren't upstairs opening your golden eyes,
Yawning, stretching, padding across the bed
Toward the tapestry stool making little cries
To let me know you're awake, and missing me.
I'm not about to hear a thump, then smile
To hear your claws tap out their melody
Across the floor—you always walked with style.
My tight grip on this pen means there's no hope
Of hearing your preemptory meow again
Calling me from the top stair as you lope
Down to fetch me, end my discipline.
For hours I sit here working on a poem.
No milk to pour, just ink. I'm on my own.

# Abstract Art

> "there is nothing in these paintings
>   that could not be changed"
>   —John Cage

Who wants St. Sebastian over the couch,
arrows sticking out of his chest,
or ladies in wigs sitting on garden swings?

Some of us looked up from our plates
of meatloaf, gazing at a still life
hanging over the dining room hutch,

knowing we'd never get to eat those grapes
shimmering next to a basket of apricots.
At my grandparent's house, I slept beneath

a portrait of Jesus having open heart surgery.
A Parisian street scene
hung over my family's first color TV

and I'd lift my eyes up during commercials
for shiny Buicks, watching the carriages
splashing down the Champs Elysees,

aware that even grown-up I could never
link arms with the two ladies in mauve dresses,
turn the corner, and slip into the past.

"No beauty, No message, No feeling, No subject"—
Reading John Cage, I understand my love
for the modern wing of the city art museum

where I used to hang out in high school.
I'd stand in the exact center
of the huge, empty room, turning

in slow circles before the canvases
of pure color, untouched by shadow
like the landscapes of eternity, and wish

I could step through their panes of light
and melt to nothingness. But soon
I'd hear the guard shuffling toward me,

and I'd go down the marble staircase
with a sigh, out past the headless Roman
clutching his stiff toga

and ride the city bus back home
to the Dutch painting where I lived
inside the rules of perspective,

ladder-back chairs crammed around a table
where human figures leaned over plates,
backs rounded, hands flashing knives.

# Cocktail Glasses

Even as a nine-months baby
the tulip shapes of thin,
enticing glasses on end tables
beckoned me. I'd drop my rattle
and crawl across the carpet
reaching for the stemmed crystal
glittering with something clear
like water, but much shinier.
The fat, magnified olive
pierced by a toothpick wrapped
brightly in red cellophane,
bobbed gently near the bottom.
I learned to stand, they say,
by grabbing a couch cushion
then pulling myself up
as I reached for the glass
until an aunt, stubbing out
a lipstick-printed cigarette
noticed me, and laughed,
lifting me up on her lap.
When I no longer ate strained
carrots with my baby spoon,
or sucked on a warm bottle,
my grandfather would save
his gin-soaked olive for me,
and I'd toddle toward him
in my organdy pinafore
trimmed with red rick-rack.
I made them laugh, they said,
my mouth puckering up,

as I chewed and swallowed
a Manhattan-soaked cherry,
but I always wanted another,
thrilled by the odd taste.
I remember staying behind
when the grown-ups filed into
the dining room for dinner
lining empty glasses in a row
along the coffee table,
admiring the sparkling stems
under the shaded lamps.
I'd practice the elegant gestures
of my grandparents and aunts,
who lived in the flat above ours.
When I was older, I'd sneak upstairs
away from my baby brothers
playing with their ABC blocks.
My grandmother took naps,
so I'd tiptoe past the gold
chiming clock on the mantelpiece
and slip into the dining room.
I'd switch on the chandelier
with its hanging prisms
that shot light everywhere,
illuminating the china cabinet
filled with a hundred glasses
or more, all of them different,
some thin as a skim of ice,
others carved deeply like jewels
but strangely made out of lead.
I liked the heavy-bottomed ones
called "Old-Fashioned" glasses,
and the tall champagne flutes,
and the hand-blown wine glasses,
and the big bells for brandy,
and the plain shot glasses

for Irish whiskey, and the tiny
sparkling doll-sized glasses
for green and orange liqueurs.
Later I hated the tumblers
for chocolate milk, the juice glasses
stamped with smiling oranges,
and the Porky Pig drinking mugs
dug from boxes of soap
after we moved from Chicago
and my father stopped drinking
for the rest of his life.

# Meditation while Cooking Soup

To throw into the boiling pot of water
peeled new potatoes and watch them roll around
under the steam reminds me I hate meanness,
how preachers say God loves the cheerful sound

of sinners thrashing in Hell's busy cauldrons.
But what of happy children snatched from arms,
left clinging to a tree, rammed by a wave
that goes back out again with houses and farms?

He loves that, too, it seems. It's punishment,
bereft parents are told by monks and priests,
imams and missionaries, while scientists
read seismic charts, study the damaged reefs,

and blame South Asia's lack of technology.
Each night on the French news by satellite,
amateur videos show the huge tsunami
advancing over the beach, ready to smite

whoever's there, like some avenging angel
determined to destroy the human race,
or part of it. Filmed from mosques and hotels,
the sea sweeps everything into its embrace—

palm trees, boats, cars, tourists, whole trains—
reminding those of us in wooden homes,
back home in Indiana, cooking dinner,
how quickly playful shouts can turn to moans.

One second you're alive, the next you're dead,
like my great-great-grandparents in Ireland,
William and Bridget Staunton, who both drowned
when the sea roared wildly across the strand

and met them at the turn of the Tooreen road
between Lough Carra and Lough Mask,
so far inland the fields stank from dead fish.
I remember walking that road, stopping to ask

stone cutters in a graveyard for directions
back to Ballinrobe, and glimpsing the sea
shining like a wand on the distant horizon.
Did it really happen? You can barely see

the shore from the road. Now I see it's true.
That old story, passed through generations,
kept alive what now camcorders show us—
one day Nature will destroy all nations.

# Beginning Poetry Writing, 1968

Tuesday, 6 P.M., we moved
Twelve desks into a circle.
A short man in corduroy
Sat next to me, biting his nails.
I was twenty. Bob was fifty—
Creased face, thin graying hair,
A pipe bulging in his pocket.
We all took turns reading poems,
Our voices shy, embarrassed.
But not Bob. He chanted,
Waved his hands, shouted.
But at what? We didn't know
For he wrote in Welsh forms
So difficult to construct
Out of syllables, rhymes,
Diphthongs, alliteration
Arranged in each quatrain,
That his words lost all sense.
Yet nothing could be changed
In his jigsaw text—
The third syllable of line four
Cross rhymed just so.
Change that, or that, or that!?
Scorn lit up his face.
He'd suck the stem of his pipe,
His eyes bright, dismissive.

At night the televised war,
The body count steadily rising,
Drove me down to the basement

Where I sat at my father's desk.
Images spilled from me then—
"Skulls fleshed over with soil"
Or "the school yard waits
For imminent invasion."
I wrote till my hand ached
On the soft yellow paper
Required for J-school classes.
I'd planned to be a reporter
But lies filled the papers.
Nothing mattered but poetry
And that stifling classroom
Where the radiator clanked
Louder than our quiet voices
And once a week I basked
In the teacher's praise. But Bob
Grew more and more tight-faced,
Angry at our bafflement,
Lecturing us at length
On his fixed, elaborate forms,
Parsing his lines, explaining
How this meant that,
Convinced we were stupid
As he reread his poems to us
Loudly, with great passion,
While our teacher winced, sighed,
And we lowered our eyes,
Nodding, keeping our mouths shut.

Once I saw him on a bus.
He got off at Lutheran Brotherhood,
The insurance company my sister
Quit out of boredom.
I knew he worked on annuities,
And I imagined him on break
Constructing his puzzle-like rhymes

While his coworkers smoked,
Drank coffee, talked of sons
Drafted, the latest protests.
Then the class ended
And I forgot him. But today,
Thirty-five years later,
Sickened by another war,
I turn off CNN
And grab *The Book of Forms,*
Browsing to calm myself,
And come across complicated
Patterns for Welsh poems.
At once the schematic stanzas
Conjure his fierce face,
And I can hear him reciting
His Englyns and Toddaids,
Totally incomprehensible,
But packed with impotent rage.

# Greed

*after Callimachus*


"Why are you chopping down my lovely trees?"
  "To build a house to feast my dearest friends."
"Where will my stag feed? My unblinking hare?"
  "Demeter, I own these fields, these forests, and these streams."

So the Goddess punished him with savage hunger.
None of the stuff he ate could satisfy
His raging belly. Twenty sweating teenagers
Served his Big Macs and twelve poured out his Cokes.
He ordered sausage pizzas by the thousands,
Buckets of chicken, barbecued ribs, and shrimp.
His gastric juices sang for more and more
And the more he ate, the more he desired to eat.
His embarrassed family declined all invitations.
"Sorry, he's gone hunting," said his son.
"He can't come, he's slightly indisposed,"
Said his wife. His daughter: "He's not home."
Imagine a hole the size of Lake Superior
Filled with herds of succulent red cattle,
Flocks of bleating sheep, fresh eggs, and fish
Leaping on the speckled backs of one another,
All flowing uselessly into his mouth
For he grew thinner with every fat swallow,
Until his skin was cellophane over bones
Stacked up like Legos ready to topple over.
His wife opened the kitchen cabinet doors
And wept. He'd eaten the sugar, the flour,
The scented birthday candles, the toothpicks,
And now she heard him shake the gerbil's cage.
He ate the gerbil, he ate the dog, he ate

The cat, he ate the mouse caught in the trap,
And when she saw him on his hands and knees
At the baseboard, trying to catch a cricket,
She sent the children to her mother's and prayed
To Jesus words like these: "Oh, dear Savior,
Please cure this man who only wanted a deck,
Jacuzzi, four-car garage, and 6,000 square feet
On seven acres to raise his beloved family
Free from drugs and inner-city youth."
Now there was nothing left at home to eat.
His teeth were aching; his belly craved
Morsels of anything, and he wandered wide
The streets of his town, rooting in the garbage,
Savoring tossed-out banana peels, stale
Cheerios in the bottoms of yellow boxes,
Dregs of salad dressing, curdled milk, gristle.
Sometimes he waited on the curb outside a feast
Of the sort he used to give, all delightful song,
And begged the guests for a scrap of this, a crumb of that.

# Dream Kitchen

A countertop installer fans
The colors on his ring of samples.
"Dolphin Grey?" "Kid Leather White?"
The mother fingers "Burnt Pecan."

Softly the child exhales the breath
Caught inside her narrow lungs;
Beneath the sink that must come out
She hears the mice whispering, "run!"

Knives nap inside stiff drawers
Ready to chop fingers or tails.
She keeps her fists tight like snails
Curled inside her sweater pockets.

Her pricked ears can hear the spell
Of the refrigerator, humming
To chill the bacon, cool the eggs.
She's seen blood inside a shell

And will not eat an egg for lunch.
Now the installer's gone to order
Big sheets of "Sea Foam Green."
She grabs her box of Cap'n Crunch.

Nuggets fly out over the bowl
Trying to escape her digging spoon.
She lets one gallop off and roll
Beneath the toaster, saved by shadow,

But the oven's going click, click,
Click, click. She might climb in,
Knees up, tilt back her chin,
And bask to death like roast beef.

What's in the cupboard? Nightmares.
The child gasps while the mother
Unlatches the door. Then she dares
A look. Mother's got the broom.

Carefully the child drinks juice,
Her goat's body trembling again
While her mother sweeps and sings
About her lovely dream kitchen

Not knowing that the evil broom
Might carry her north or south,
That the dustpan's yawning mouth
Opens for bites of dirt or kid.

# Little Sonata for Early November

*for Walter Bricht*

Under the piano stool's threadbare velvet
Hand-written music fades on yellowing sheets.
Forced from his job in Vienna by Hitler,
My neighbor's first husband, a composer,
Taught where he could, taking on pupils
In France, then England, then West Virginia.
Once he played piano duets with Ravel.
A famous conductor performed his symphony.
But now his music, piled up since 1970
When she watched him die in the hospital,
His face twisted blue by emphysema,
Worries her. Who will play his C Major
Flute sonata? she asks. His works for viola
And violin, his brilliant compositions
So full of melodies and balanced themes
Could disappear. And so I give advice
About copies and libraries, tell her to call
This professor or that one, and she nods
Then goes back to doing what she was doing
When she stopped to talk, raking the leaves
Spread like golden notes across her lawn.
And I go on with my walk, but now my head
Swells with harmonies I've never heard,
Resounding piano keys and plucked strings
Muting the chirp of crickets and crackle of leaves.

# Cimetière Virtual

*"Une association de retraites de Dijon a ouvert
sur Internet un cimetière virtuel"*

My father's buried under
A soundless roof of snow.
His tiny marker's hidden
In Ft. Snelling Cemetary
Where an icy fog drifts
Across from the airport,
And no one visits him
Or the thousands of others
Lost to sight all winter.
And so I've created
My own *Cimetière Virtual*
For him, but also for you,
Should you wish to bury
Your lost loved one
Here in my cyberspace.
Click on the Home Page
And create your weather
To fit the day's sadness—
Clouds and stinging sleet
For deep, early grief,
Or shafts of bright sunshine
For more mellow reflection.
And here's the large menu
Of poetic locations. Choose
This stunning view of the sea
And brood on the dazzle
Of immortality,
Or soothe your sorrow
By counting the wild waves.
Yet you might prefer

This rustic churchyard
Where a few sheep graze
Among moss-covered tombstones
Picturesquely tilted.
And I offer many trees—
Classic yews, Italian cypress.
My gossamer cemetery
Offers what the real one lacked
On that May morning
When the plastic bouquets
Brightened the mowed plots,
And I stared at a dandelion,
Afraid to imagine
The uninhabited skulls
Lying below my feet.
Here, sitting at home,
I can easily download
The beloved voice, saying
Whatever I wish to hear,
And call up the smiling face.
Come through the iron gate
Of the Chateau Le Marais
With me right now, and see
A young man in uniform
Gazing down at his bride.
Swans cross the silvery pond.
The sky's blue forever
In this perfected space.

# Immortal Sofa

"I sing the sofa"
—William Cowper

When I see sofas hauled from student dumps,
and set out on the curb in heavy showers,
I know it's spring. Time to clear out of here,
start life again with nothing but a suitcase.
But here's my house. Yes, I admit I'm staying.
My sofa won't be going out the door.
Instead I join the cat asleep on the afghan,
warm my hands on a hot mug of tea,
and remember my mother-in-law's rowhouse
in Baltimore, crammed with quilted armchairs,
glass ashtrays deep as birdbaths, cattails
dried to mauve, stuck in a Chinese vase.
No wonder I vowed never to own anything,
no Turkish carpets, lamps, or cabinets,
especially not a long, three-cushion sofa
covered in protective dull green serge,
antimacassars of yellow lace on the armrests.
Ah, but my mother-in-law secretly longed
to buy an off-white love seat at Sears
and here was her chance to finally give away
a ten-year-old sofa in perfect condition.
Too poor to refuse, my husband and I
U-Hauled the sofa down to Virginia,
where it mildewed in storage for a year
until we found a larger place to live.
We used to lounge, legs tangled, after work,
drinking gimlets, talking about dream cities.
Slowly the sofa rose up, carrying us
out the sliding doors of our apartment.
Far below we'd see the twinkling lights

of Richmond, some barges on the James,
mowed sweeps of battlefields and cemeteries
getting smaller as the sofa flew higher,
rushing along the highways of air, headed
for the Andes, or the jungles of Brazil.
And sometimes we'd be set down, gently,
on the outskirts of Cuzco or Asuncion
dazed by herds of llama, or red cattle
that parted to sweep past our magic sofa.
Or we might float over a foaming waterfall
inches above a rainbow, giddy and dizzy,
scared but safe on our familiar cushions.
But when we finally moved to California,
owners of beds, tables, desks, and chairs
and boxes of things of all sorts and sizes,
we took the dirty cover off the sofa,
discovering chartreuse satin brocade.
Yet though it looked shiny and brand-new
against the ugly black-and-white swirled carpet
of our rented bungalow in Hell,
the sofa couldn't fly under the weight
of two hearts heavy as the redwood
sliced and polished into our coffee table.
We'd stumble home from work with umbrellas,
turn the cold knob on the gas space-heater,
then head to bed. So maybe we were dreaming
suddenly to find new jobs under palms
in Arizona, my mother-in-law
arriving to sit on her old sofa, shrunken
as if she'd stepped from a fun-house mirror,
remarking on the good quality of the fabric.
Then she was dead, outlived by the sofa,
which moved into this house in Indiana,
barely fitting through the angled hallway.
Clawed by cats, flea-sprayed, recovered
in blue velvet, the sofa sags and dips

from indentations of spines and buttocks
of all the people who've ever sat here
to talk, or read, or put their feet up,
one warm impression after another
loosening, crushing, squashing, flattening.
Once we tried to buy a stylish sofa
but though the workmen unhinged the door
and laid it flat in the snow, they couldn't
wedge the new one inside, and took it back,
leaving this one safe for years to come.
How many books have I read sitting here?
How many times have I returned from trips
glad to fling myself on these battered cushions?
If ever I get to wander the roomy clouds
of Heaven, my golden cup of nectar
brimming over, I'll look for my sofa.
I think I'll find it far from the incense
and the loud hosannas, a quiet spot
for those who'd rather doze a bit, and dream,
than sing loudly with the choirs of angels.

# Notes

All the animals in "Nineteenth-Century Animals" can be found in Marianne North's memoir, *Recollections of a Happy Life*.

The ending of "Poem on a Forbidden Subject" echoes the ending of Baudelaire's poem "L'Etranger"—*"J'aime les nuages . . . les nuages que passent . . . la-bas . . . la-bas . . . les merveilleux nuages!"* Thank you French teachers!

The "Tale of Hermann Goertz" is loosely based on Hermann Goertz's life and death as found in *The Shamrock and the Swastika: German Espionage in Ireland in World War II* by Carolle J. Carter.

# Illinois Poetry Series

*Laurence Lieberman, Editor*

MAURA STANTON was born in Evanston, Illinois and grew up in Chicago and Peoria. She received her BA from the University of Minnesota and her MFA from the University of Iowa. Her first book of poetry, *Snow On Snow,* was selected by Stanley Kunitz for the Yale Series of Younger Poets Award. Her second collection, *Cries of Swimmers,* was published by the University of Utah Press in 1984. Each of these titles has been reprinted in the Carnegie Mellon Classic Contemporary Series. *Tales of the Supernatural* was published by David R. Godine in 1988. Carnegie Mellon published *Life Among the Trolls* in 1998 and *Glacier Wine* in 2001. Her novel, *Molly Companion,* was set in South America and reprinted in Spanish as *Rio Abajo. The Country I Come From,* stories about growing up in the Midwest, appeared from Milkweed Editions in 1988, and *Do Not Forsake Me, Oh My Darling,* a collection of short stories, won the Richard Sullivan Prize for 2002 and was published by the University of Notre Dame Press. *Cities in the Sea,* a collection of short stories, won the Michigan Literary Award, and was published by the University of Michigan Press in 2003. She is a professor of English at Indiana University where she teaches in the MFA Program in Creative Writing.

The University of Illinois Press
is a founding member of the
Association of American University Presses.

---

Composed in 10.5/14 Adobe Garamond
with Avenir display
by Celia Shapland
at the University of Illinois Press
Designed by Kelly Gray
Manufactured by Thomson-Shore, Inc.

University of Illinois Press
1325 South Oak Street
Champaign, IL 61820-6903
www.press.uillinois.edu